GOURMET VINEGARS

HOW TO MAKE AND COOK WITH THEM

By Marsha Peters Johnson

Mark worder;
see index
pg 60

Design Consultant: Darrel Streets
Original Cover Art: Char Parks
Editorial Staff: Cynthia Fischborn
            Heather Kibbey
            Cheryl Long

ISBN# 0-914667-10-6

Printed in the United States of America

Published by:
Culinary Arts Ltd.
P.O. Box 2157
Lake Oswego, Oregon 97035

Books by Culinary Arts Ltd.:

Gourmet Vinegars: How To Make And Cook With Them
Gourmet Mustards: How To Make And Cook With Them
Easy Microwave Preserving
Classic Liqueurs:
        The Art Of Making And Cooking With Liqueurs
How To Make Danish Fruit Liqueurs

Publisher's catalog available upon request.

TABLE OF CONTENTS

ABOUT THE AUTHOR

Marsha Peters Johnson founded and operated the firm, **Oregon's Own Gourmet Vinegars**, specializing in the production of a wide range of flavors. Together with her husband, Paul, she produced thousands of bottles each year. Marsha and Paul have two sons and a daughter.

ACKNOWLEDGMENTS

To the three fine women who made this project even imaginable: Cheryl Long, Heather Kibbey and Cynthia Fischborn. Special thanks to my vinegar-loving husband and family for their capacity to eat my home-cooked experiments. And lastly, to my children, for sleeping soundly while I wrote.

INTRODUCTION

I discovered vinegars in Europe as I ate my way through 13 countries one year. Later, finding myself at loose ends, I finally connected the superb Oregon berry crops with an excellent white wine vinegar to start my own business, **Oregon's Own Gourmet Vinegars**. The success story continued! My company flourished and, by 1986, I had completed negotiations with the prestigious Oregon firm, Heins Honey, for the sale of my business. With Heins' interest in expanding its line to include a wider variety of quality gourmet foods, my vinegars are now reaching a wider market under the label of **Oregon Trails Gourmet Vinegars**.

Over the years, it has been my pleasure to develop a wide variety of ways to use gourmet vinegars. In this book, you will find my secrets for both making and cooking with the whole range of exciting flavors. I hope you love or learn to love vinegars as much as I do.

Marsha Peters Johnson

"A loaf of bread," the Walrus said,
"Is what we chiefly need:
Pepper and vinegar besides
Are very good indeed."

Lewis Carroll
Through the Looking-Glass

BASICS OF
VINEGAR
MAKING

BASICS OF VINEGAR MAKING

EQUIPMENT:

You will probably be able to find everything you'll need in your own kitchen cupboards. The basic rule in all vinegar making is to avoid any contact between the vinegar and certain metals, such as aluminum. Since vinegar is such an acidic substance, it will leach the metal molecules from a metal pot, bowl or spoon. Be careful to use only plastic or glass bottles for storing and aging the vinegars. In addition, make sure that you have tight fitting lids for those jugs, jars or bottles as your sweet fruit and spice vinegars can draw 'friends' of the unwelcome variety.

VINEGAR MAKING EQUIPMENT:

Several large (½ gallon) plastic tubs for mixing and aging, with tight fitting lids
Plastic spoons
Plastic strainer or colander
Glass or plastic measuring cups; 1, 2 and 4-cup sizes
Plastic funnel, sized to fit small bottle openings
Cheesecloth or fine cotton cloth for straining

EQUIPMENT FOR BOTTLING:

Bottles or glass jars with lids; 6, 8, 12 or 16-ounce size
Screw tops for bottles, metal with plastic liners or plastic lids
Corks for bottles, brand new, please do not use recycled ones
Wax for sealing corks, half paraffin and half beeswax
Labels
Ribbon, run under wax or tie on recipe
Ground spices or oils for mixing with the wax

PREPARATION OF EQUIPMENT:

Everything needs to be completely free of grease or other contamination before beginning the mixing of the vinegars. To do this, wash all the items in hot soapy water, then rinse with very hot, almost boiling water. You may also accomplish the same 'squeaky clean' equipment by putting everything through a full dishwasher cycle, which is definitely easier.

VINEGARS:

Since you won't actually be making the vinegar itself, it is important to learn about what varieties are available at your local supermarkets and the vast differences between these types. The following is a list of vinegars commonly found in a medium-sized city:

Plain white distilled
Apple cider
Red and white wine *
Malt
Barley
Rice
Balsamic

Strength of vinegar is very important. The acetic acid content of vinegars varies from 4 to 7 percent, with the standard being 5 percent.

Acetic acid content is also referred to by 'grains', for example, a 5% acetic acid content vinegar is also known as a 50 grain vinegar. The whole business refers to the amount of water the vinegar is diluted with; for example, 50 grain vinegar is 50% vinegar, 50% water. The advantage of seeking out a higher acetic acid content is that it helps keep food fresher longer, acting as a better preservative, which is what vinegar really is in the first place. Depending on what the vinegar is made from, it can have many different qualities. White distilled vinegar, in my opinion, has hardly any taste other than sour, and is fine for making certain things like pickles, where you want only sour. However, if you are seeking the best in vinegars, look to the wine vinegars made from top quality wines. The taste and body of the grapes will shine through your finished bottles and you will be more satisfied with the results. Read the labels carefully and see if you can determine the vinegar's origin, acidic level and place of manufacture.

* See page 62 for mail-order resource.

I have come to discover that, given a fair chance, any vinegar, excluding distilled white vinegar, can lend a pleasing quality and aroma to a final product. I do enjoy using a strong white wine vinegar for most of my concoctions, but have expanded my taste over the past five years to allow room for the slightly pungent, full fruity bouquet of apple cider vinegars. Garlic tends to blend exceptionally well with this staple of the pantry, as well as onion flavors. Don't be afraid to try just about any combination of vinegars, either, as mixing a white wine with an equal part of rice vinegar can be delightful mixed with fresh herbs, a dollop of lovely pale golden green olive oil and seasoned to taste.

The white wine varieties do act as the best base, however, for the showy fresh fruit and vegetable colors that are extracted during aging. For home use and gift giving, take these factors into your consideration and planning. Balsamic vinegars are still expensive, usually imported and are generally of such a high caliber in flavor that it would be a crime to try to add anything other than good olive oil and seasonings. I have recently acquired some malt vinegars and have had moderate success in playing with additions of nasturtium seeds and flowers, making for a welcome peppery taste that is even good over the traditional fish and chips. Barley vinegar I have not come into close friendship with yet and if you have success with it, please let me know!

Vinegars, in particular the wine varieties, are made from good quality drinking wines. It is not just 'good wine gone bad': as a matter of fact, it is nearly impossible to turn out a decent vinegar by letting good wine sour. What you end up with is sour wine, not good vinegar. Vinegar is the result of careful introduction of friendly bacteria into wine, monitored under carefully controlled temperatures and environment. Home-made vinegars use a 'mother' which is a rather nasty looking stuff resembling a thick jelly-like material, which, if carefully mixed with wine, will turn out a beautiful vinegar. However, it is a chancy business and you're better off buying the vinegar already made at the store.

SHELF LIFE OF FINISHED VINEGAR:

Flavored vinegars will keep up to 18 months, possibly longer, if stored in proper containers in a cool dark place. Some fruit sugars, like strawberry or blueberry, tend to carmelize after a while and turn slightly brown, which isn't as attractive as a clear red or violet liquid. These two vinegars should be used up in 3 months to avoid this problem. Since high acid content vinegar is often used as a preservative itself, spoiling just isn't a problem. Usually, you'll end up wishing you'd made twice as much because it disappears so quickly.

BOTTLES:

This is the place to use your creative ideas for containers and finishing touches, as long as you avoid any metal containers or lids. Glass bottles or jars, special decanters with plastic lids, rubber rings, glass tops or corks are all appropriate for vinegars when properly scrubbed and sterilized with boiling water. A bottle brush can be handy for cleaning out re-used bottles. You can also use plastic containers if they are of food grade quality. Of course, then you miss out on the treat of seeing the beautiful colors and/or ingredients of the vinegars, which are half the reason for making them!

To use corks for the top, buy only top quality corks from a winery supply or beer making supply store and inspect them carefully for signs of decay or imperfection. After inserting them into the bottle mouth, finish by dipping in wax, preferably a mixture of half paraffin to half beeswax for easy peeling later on. The melted wax may be improved by adding ground spices such as cinnamon or strong oils like oil of cloves. This gives a nice warm tone and scent to the finished product. Then with a ribbon tied around the neck holding a special recipe for that vinegar, you're ready for holiday gift-giving, house-warming or birthday parties.

FRUITS, FLAVORING SPICES, HERBS AND VEGETABLES:

In my business I select fresh top quality berries direct from rich Oregon fields to make my vinegar nectars. In your area the produce available to you may be different. Just remember, buy the best quality produce you can find, as fresh as possible. Frozen produce is also useful and makes good quality vinegars. Most of your spices will be dried. Herbs should be fresh, especially if you plan to leave them in the bottles. Dried herbs are satisfactory but need a little help in heating and straining before bottling. As the quantities of vinegar required for vinegar making are not large, you can supply yourself with a full pantry of specialty flavors for a relatively small investment in raw materials.

Certain fruits and vegetables need to be peeled, chopped, mashed, smashed, blended, or heated to release all their flavors into the vinegar. We'll deal with that in the individual recipes for vinegars that follow this chapter.

AGING TIME:

Certain recipes that require heating will be ready for use at once, but the majority of vinegars in this book require about a month to fully develop their unique flavors. I believe in cold processing as opposed to hot processing. Treating the fruit or herbs gently and combining them with vinegar in its prime makes a great finished product, full of the natural vitamins and nutrients leached from the fruit or herbs during the aging process. Minimum aging times are indicated in the vinegar recipes.

I have called for plastic tubs with tight lids to be used in the aging process. Food grade quality plastic does not affect the flavor or taste at all and turns out a very fine vinegar. Glass is also good for aging, i.e., quart jars as long as the lid is not metal! The best flavor, however, can be obtained by using wood casks. These can be obtained from wine or beer making outlets.

STRAINING:

While siphoning works well in certain vinegars, other vinegars need not be strained at all, only bottled at mixing time. However, there are many vinegars which need to be strained several times through double layers of cheesecloth inside a plastic strainer to eliminate fruit/herb/vegetable pieces and leave a perfectly clear, stunningly colored liquid for the bottles.

Using two layers of cheesecloth inside your plastic colander or strainer, pour your aged vinegar mix into the strainer gently, catching the liquid under the strainer in a clean plastic tub or large bowl. You may need to strain several times using clean cheesecloth each time and rinsing the tubs or glass bowls each time until you obtain a perfectly clear liquid.

EQUIVALENT LIQUID MEASURES

3 teaspoons	=	1 tablespoon
2 tablespoons	=	1 ounce
5$\frac{1}{3}$ tablespoons	=	$\frac{1}{3}$ cup
8 ounces	=	1 cup
16 tablespoons	=	1 cup
2 cups	=	1 pint
16 ounces	=	1 pint
2 pints	=	1 quart
32 ounces	=	1 quart
4 quarts	=	1 gallon

METRIC CONVERSION

1 milliliter	=	.034 fluid ounces
1 liter	=	33.8 fluid ounces or 4.2 cups
1 fluid ounce	=	29.56 milliliters
1 fluid cup	=	236 milliliters
1 fluid quart	=	946 milliliters or .946 liters
1 teaspoon	=	5 milliliters
1 tablespoon	=	15 milliliters

MAKING
GOURMET
VINEGARS

his chapter will help you set up your own complete pantry of specialty vinegars. Before long, you will be choosing gourmet vinegars to replace regular vinegar or lemon juice in your favorite recipes. The subtle difference will be evident as your barbecue sauces, salad dressings and marinades become tastier. They will add the gourmet touch that is the signature of a truly good cook. People will start asking for your recipes and will be surprised to learn the difference is the vinegar! Do them a favor and give them a bottle of your favorite with the requested recipe attached.

RECIPE FOR BASIC BERRY VINEGARS

Of all the fruits, berries are perhaps the easiest to use in vinegar-making as they contain so much juice and don't need to be peeled or pitted. Here in Oregon the berries are huge, juicy and perfect for good vinegar. If you can get fresh, so much the better; if not, frozen will do, but be sure to use frozen berries with no sugar added.

Many people ask me what my favorite vinegar is and I always say "Raspberry". Looking through the recipe section of this book made me realize that there are very few foods that wouldn't be enhanced by the addition of this out-standing vinegar. The following basic recipe can be made with any of the berries listed below.

1 to 1½ pounds ripe berries, washed and drained (see below)
1 quart white vinegar*, preferably 5% acidity or higher

In a large glass bowl, prepare berries as indicated below. Stir in the vinegar. Pour into jar(s) for aging. (If using more than one jar, be sure to divide berries and vinegar equally.) Cover with plastic wrap secured by rubber bands. Let age in a cool, dark place about 3 to 4 weeks, then strain through cheesecloth and plastic strainer until clear. Pour into bottles and seal. Use within 18 months.

*For the best color effect, use the white wine vinegar. You may substitute red wine vinegar for a nice full-bodied taste.

VARIATIONS:

Any of the following berries may be used in the Basic Recipe:

- Blackberries: 1 pound, crushed well
- Blueberries: 1 pound, ground in a blender with about ⅓ cup of the vinegar
- Cranberries: 1 pound, ground in a blender with about ⅓ cup of the vinegar

- Currants: 1 pound fresh, ground in a blender with about $^1/_3$ cup of the vinegar
- Huckleberries: 1 pound, ground in a blender with about $^1/_3$ cup of the vinegar
- Loganberries: 1 pound, crushed well
- Marionberries: 1 pound, crushed well
- Raspberries: 1 to 1 ½ pounds, crushed well
- Strawberries: 1 pound, hulled and crushed well

RECIPE FOR BASIC FRUIT VINEGARS

In general, making fruit vinegars takes a little more preparation than herb, spice or berry vinegars. However, the results are quite pleasant and interesting and add something to foods that can't be obtained any other way. Makes about 1 quart.

1 to 2 lbs. ripe fruit; washed and drained (see list below)
1 quart white or red wine vinegar, 5 to 7% acidity

Combine prepared fruit and vinegar in a large glass bowl. Pour into glass jar(s), (if using more than 1 jar be sure to divide fruit and vinegar equally), for aging. Store in a cool dark place for at least 1 month to properly age and mellow flavors.

FRUIT VARIATIONS:

Apricot: One pound apricots. Pit but do not peel. Grind in a meat grinder or chop very fine to release juice.

Cherries: One pound cherries, pitted and ground in blender with $^1/_3$ cup of the vinegar.

Kiwi: Eight to nine kiwi fruit, peeled and finely chopped. A very unique color and flavor.

Lemon, Lime or Orange: Three of any fruit. Thinly peel fruit, being careful not to include the bitter white layer. Finely chop the peel. Squeeze fruit to extract juice and add juice and pulp to vinegar.   **Tip:** When bottling, add a few fresh spirals of peel to each final bottle for color.

Nectarine: About four to five nectarines, pitted. Chop into bits.

Papaya or Mango: One large or two small fruits. Peel, seed and mash well.

Peach: One pound peaches, peeled, pitted and chopped into bits.

Pear: One pound pears, peeled, cored and chopped into bits.

Persimmon: One pound persimmons, fully ripe and soft. Discard stems, coarsely chop and save juice. Makes about two cups of pulp and juice. Gorgeous color.

Pineapple: One-half fresh pineapple. Remove peel, discard. Finely chop fruit. Add any juice to vinegar when mixing.

Rhubarb: One pound rhubarb. Finely chop. In saucepan heat rhubarb with ¼ cup water until it comes to a boil. Let cool before continuing.

Tangerine: Six or seven tangerines. Peel three tangerines. Finely chop the peel. Squeeze the juice from all the tangerines. Add the peel, juice and pulp to the vinegar.

Watermelon: About three pounds. Remove skin and green rind; discard. Mash remaining watermelon meat, including the seeds.   **Tip:** Add a few whole seeds to each final bottle for color.

RECIPE FOR BASIC HERB VINEGARS

*Herb vinegars are the most widely distributed and best known
vinegars today. Large companies produce them commercially
but they are simple and inexpensive to make at home. In my
mind's eye, I can see that busy housewife who saw a way to
save time and threw a handful of green herbs into the vinegar
vat long ago. Lucky us! Makes 1 quart.*

1 generous handful finely chopped fresh herbs* (see
   list below)
1 qt. good vinegar, any kind with 5% to 7% acidity

Basil (green or purple), Chives and Flowers, Cilantro, Dill
Weed, Mint, Parsley, Rosemary, Sage, Tarragon, Thyme or
any other herb you have on hand. Combine herbs and
vinegar. Age in covered glass jar(s) for one month in a cool
dark place.

*DRIED HERB VARIATION: You can substitute dried
herbs, using 2 to 3 tablespoons per quart. Increase the
aging time by 2 weeks. To cut the aging time down to a
week; gently heat the vinegar and add the dried herbs.
Cool, bottle and age as above. Strain through cheesecloth
until clear and bottle.

Tip: Use one or several kinds of herbs as your taste
dictates. Some suggestions are Basil-Mint or Dill-Chives
For a gourmet touch add a sprig of the herb of your choice
to the final bottle.

RECIPE FOR BASIC SPICE VINEGARS

*Perfect for pickles, marinades or coolers. For vinegar in a hurry, use the **Hot Process Method** to release immediately the essence of the spices. You may prefer, as I do, the slower but simpler **Cold Process Method.***

1 qt. vinegar, any kind
dried spices, see list below

SPICE VARIATIONS:

2 to 3 Tbsp. whole anise seeds
2 to 3 sticks cinnamon
2 to 3 Tbsp. whole cloves
2 to 3 Tbsp. peppercorns

Hot Process: Gently heat vinegar in stainless steel pot on stovetop or in a large glass bowl in the microwave. Add spices to hot vinegar. Cool and strain. Bottle and label at once. (No aging time necessary with this method. Vinegar may be used immediately.)

Cold Process: Put spices into bottles with cool vinegar. Label, then age for four weeks before using.

Tip: Add a few whole spices to each final bottle for decoration.

RECIPE FOR BASIC VEGETABLE VINEGARS

These are perhaps the most unusual vinegars. The flavors are released when the tough fibers are broken down through chopping and mashing. Makes 1 quart.

Ripe vegetables (see list below)
1 qt. white or red wine vinegar, 5% or 7% acidity

VEGETABLE VARIATIONS:

Use 1 of the following:
6 to 8 garlic cloves, peeled and mashed flat*
2 to 3 bunches of green onions, thinly sliced
1 lb. green, red or yellow peppers, seeded and chopped
3 to 4 hot peppers, seeded and sliced
1 lb. sweet onions, peeled and sliced
½ lb. shallots, peeled and chopped

Prepare vegetables as directed and mix with vinegar. Store in covered jars and age 4 weeks. Remove vegetables by straining through cheesecloth until clear, then bottle.

Tip: Place several pieces of fresh vegetable, such as pepper rings or garlic cloves, in final bottles.

*It is possible to bottle garlic vinegar in one step by adding peeled garlic cloves, cut into halves, to the final bottles with the vinegar.

INTRODUCTION TO FLOWER VINEGARS

Very special are those vinegars that are flavored and colored with flowers. In many other countries, people eat flowers of different varieties, and regard them as casually as you and I would a carrot. If you would care to experiment with flowers, do not use those that have been chemically treated for insects, mold, or fungus. Also avoid flowers that are near other bushes and plants that have been similarly treated. Of course, do not use poisonous flowers or leaves.

The most common flower vinegar is made using nasturtium flowers, the seed of which is often compared to a caper. You can immerse whole or chopped flowers in vinegar bottles for a stunning effect or combine them with other flavoring agents such as spices, peppers or herbs. Nasturtiums have a peppery taste, which is quite pleasant. Other flowers that you can use include violets, roses, various herb flowers, and chive blossoms.

RECIPE FOR BASIC FLOWER VINEGAR

1 qt. fine white wine vinegar
1 to 2 generous handfuls of flowers, thoroughly washed
    and drained

Combine in large 1 quart glass jar and cover tightly. Age 3 months, then strain and use.

INTRODUCTION TO MIXED VINEGARS

A mixed vinegar is one made with a combination of flavoring agents that produces a unique and lively blend. To experiment on your own, start with your favorite flavors. After your first taste of success, you will grow bolder and even more creative.

As a general rule of thumb, remember that heat comes ahead of cold. In other words, if one of the ingredients must be heated to release its full flavor and color, do so first and then combine with vinegar. Then add the cold-processed portion and put into plastic containers to age. If more than one ingredient must be heated, do them at the same time. If several or all of the ingredients will be cold-processed, do everything together. It may look like a mixed-up crazy-quilt initially, but given a month of aging time to smooth the flavors, you'll find a treasure after straining.

SWEET BASIL WITH BLUEBERRY VINEGAR

Use the purple basil with the purple-violet blueberries for a lovely flavor and color. Makes 1 quart.

1 qt. fine white wine vinegar
1 lb. fresh or frozen blueberries, pulverized **or** ground in a
   blender with 1/3 cup of the vinegar
1 good handful of sweet purple basil, leaves and stems,
   finely chopped

Combine all ingredients. Store in a covered aging container in a cool dark place for 4 weeks. Strain through layers of cheesecloth, then bottle and label. Cap with corks and wax, or use plastic screw-on lids.

Tip: Add a few whole blueberries to final bottle(s) for color.

RASPBERRY SPICE VINEGAR

This is a wonderful sweet clear red nectar with zip! Makes 1 quart.

1 to 1½ lbs. ripe red raspberries
1 qt. fine white wine vinegar
1 Tbsp. whole cloves, allspice **or** cracked peppercorns

Mash berries well with wooden spoon. If you prefer, use a blender or food processor, adding ⅓ cup of the vinegar. Combine berries and vinegar in a large bowl. Add spices and stir well with plastic or wooden spoon. Pour into aging container. Cover, age in a cool dark place for 4 to 6 weeks. Strain through layers of cheesecloth until clear, then bottle and label. Seal with corks dipped in wax or use plastic screw-on caps.

STRAWBERRY WITH SPICE VINEGAR

Make strawberry vinegars in small quantities and use them within three months as they have a tendency to carmelize and turn a brownish color. Delicious mixed with sour cream and candied ginger as a dip for fresh fruit. Makes 1 quart.

1 lb. ripe red strawberries, hulled and mashed
1 tsp. ground nutmeg
1 qt. white **or** red wine vinegar
several 2 to 3 inch cinnamon sticks

Mix berries, nutmeg and vinegar together in a large glass bowl. Pour into aging container, adding cinnamon sticks. Seal tightly and age in a cool dark place for 4 weeks. Strain through layers of cheesecloth until clear. Bottle in three to four 6 or 8-ounce glass bottles. Label and cap with corks dipped in wax or screw-on plastic lids.

APRICOT WITH ALLSPICE VINEGAR

Pleasingly sweet with a bite of its own, this apricot vinegar is nicely showcased with a touch of spice. Makes 1 quart.

1 lb. ripe juicy apricots, pitted and chopped
1 Tbsp. whole allspice, slightly crushed
1 qt. white **or** red wine vinegar

Combine all ingredients in a large glass bowl. Pour into aging container; seal tightly. Age in a cool dark place for 4 weeks, then strain through layers of cheesecloth until clear. Pour into three to four 6 or 8-ounce glass bottles. Label and cap tightly with corks dipped in wax or screw-on lids.

PEACH WITH ANISE SEED VINEGAR

A pale salmon-colored vinegar with a slight licorice aroma that is perfect for fruit salad dressings or gifting. Makes 1 quart.

1 lb. ripe peaches, peeled, pitted and chopped
1 Tbsp. anise seeds, slightly crushed
1 qt. white wine vinegar

Combine all ingredients in a large bowl, stirring well. Pour into aging container and seal tightly. Age four weeks in a dark cool place, then strain through layers of cheesecloth until clear. Pour into three to four 6 or 8-ounce glass bottles. Label and cap with corks dipped in wax or plastic screw-on lids.

TANGERINE & CINNAMON VINEGAR

A lovely, light orange vinegar with a spicy taste. Makes 1 quart.

6 to 7 tangerines
1 qt. white wine vinegar
1 Tbsp. of your favorite whole spice such as cinnamon,
    allspice **or** cloves

Remove and finely chop the tangerine peel. Squeeze pulp to extract juice. Combine vinegar, peel, juice and spice in a large glass bowl. Pour into covered aging container and store in a cool, dark place for 6 weeks. Strain through layers of cheesecloth, then bottle and label. Cap with corks and wax, or use screw-on plastic lids. Label and use within 12 months.

Tip: Add a thin spiral of tangerine peel to each bottle with several whole spices.

MIXED HERBS & SPICE VINEGAR

Limited only by your imagination. Makes 1 quart.

1 generous handful of your favorite fresh herb
1 qt. fine white **or** red wine **or** apple cider vinegar
1 Tbsp. of your favorite dried whole spice, such as allspice,
    cinnamon stick, cloves, **or** grated fresh ginger root

Finely chop herb. Mix with vinegar and spices in aging container. Seal tightly and age for 4 weeks. Strain through layers of cheesecloth until clear, then bottle and label. Seal with corks dipped in wax or use screw-on plastic lids.

Tip: Add fresh sprigs of herbs and whole spices as appropriate.

MINT WITH CLOVE VINEGAR

This spicy cool green vinegar is perfect for marinating leg of lamb or ribs for barbecuing. Makes 1 quart.

1 qt. fine white wine vinegar
1 generous handful of mint leaves and stems, finely
   chopped, almost pureed.
1 Tbsp. of your favorite spices, such as whole cloves,
   allspice **or** fresh ground ginger

Combine all ingredients in a large glass bowl. Store in a covered aging container in a cool dark place for 4 weeks. Strain through layers of cheesecloth until clear; then bottle and label. Seal with corks and wax, or use plastic screw-on lids.

Tip: Add a fresh sprig of mint and 1 to 2 whole cloves to final bottles.

PEPPERS & SPICE VINEGAR

Sweet bell peppers lend themselves to an addition of spices. This makes a delicious salad dressing vinegar. Makes 1 quart.

2 to 3 large bell peppers, red, green **or** yellow, seeded,
   cored and finely chopped **or** grated
1 Tbsp. allspice, cloves, grated fresh ginger root **or** a 3-
   inch stick of cinnamon
1 qt. fine white wine vinegar

Combine all ingredients in a large glass bowl. Pour into a plastic aging container, sealing tightly. Age in a cool dark place for 4 weeks. Strain through layers of cheesecloth until clear, then bottle and label. Seal bottles with corks and wax or plastic screw lids.

Tip: Add 1 to 2 whole allspice or cloves and thin ring of pepper to each bottle for garnish.

CHIVES & CHILI VINEGAR

A gorgeous vinegar, blending the hot taste of peppers with the cool bite of chives. Makes 1 quart.

1 qt. white **or** red wine vinegar
3 to 4 hot red **or** green peppers, carefully seeded and
    coarsely chopped
3 to 4 Tbsp. minced chives
6 to 8 whole chive flowers

Mix vinegar, peppers, minced chives and half of the flowers in a plastic aging container and seal tightly. Age for 4 weeks. Strain through layers of cheesecloth until clear. Place a pepper ring or two and 1 or 2 fresh chive flowers in three 8-ounce glass bottles. Fill with strained vinegar. Label and cap with corks dipped in wax or regular screw-on plastic lids.

GREEN ONIONS & PEPPERCORN VINEGAR

This delicate green vinegar makes a fine salad dressing. Just add fresh herbs, a dollop of olive oil and a dash of salt. Makes 1 quart.

2 to 3 bunches of green onions, washed, trimmed, and
    finely chopped
1 Tbsp. green peppercorns, crushed
1 qt. white **or** red wine vinegar

Combine all ingredients in a large glass bowl. Pour into aging container and seal tightly. Age in cool dark place for 4 weeks. Strain through layers of cheesecloth until clear. Pour into three to four 6 or 8-ounce glass bottles. Label and cap tightly with corks dipped in wax or screw-on plastic lids.

DILLED GARLIC VINEGAR

This is a very easy recipe for the beginning vinegar maker since the aging and bottling is done in one step.

6 to 9 whole garlic cloves
sprigs of fresh dill weed, thoroughly washed
1 qt. fine white **or** red wine vinegar

Cut garlic cloves in half lengthwise. Add 4 to 6 garlic halves and 1 to 2 sprigs dill weed to three 8-ounce bottles. Fill with vinegar; seal with corks and wax or plastic screw lids. Label and age 4 weeks before using.

DILLED ONION VINEGAR

The full-bodied flavors of onion and dill make this easy to prepare vinegar sparkle. Economical to make. Makes 1 quart.

1 large onion, peeled and sliced into rings about ¼ inch
    thick
sprigs of fresh dill weed
1 qt. white **or** red wine vinegar

Divide onion rings between four 6-ounce bottles. Add 2 to 3 sprigs of dill weed to each bottle and fill with vinegar. Cap with corks dipped in wax or plastic screw lids. Label and age for 4 weeks.

ONION & PEPPERS VINEGAR

Here is a beautiful vinegar to see and smell. The final color depends upon the peppers you choose. Makes 1 quart.

¾ lb. sweet onion, diced, chopped **or** sliced into thin rings, with **or** without skins
2 to 3 bell peppers, red, yellow **or** green, seeded, cored and coarsely grated
1 qt. fine white vinegar

Combine all ingredients in a large glass bowl. Pour into aging container. Seal tightly and store in a cool dark place for 4 weeks. Strain through layers of cheesecloth until clear. Pour into glass bottles, seal and label.

Tip: Add a thin onion ring and pepper ring to decorate.

"... four persons are wanted to make a good salad:
a spendthrift for oil,
a miser for vinegar,
a counsellor for salt,
and a madman to stir it all up."

Abraham Hayward

COOKING
WITH
GOURMET
VINEGARS

uring the last three-and-a-half years, many people have asked me how I got started with gourmet vinegars. I have thought about this a great deal and there seems to be one simple reason: I love to eat! I have found that vinegar is the secret to better tasting foods.

Vinegar is what I call a "common denominator" ingredient. It can be used in everything from appetizers to drinks. And with the addition of different vinegars you can have an endless variety of flavors.

The recipes that follow were developed from a lifetime of cooking with vinegar, a love of fine food and my culinary curiosity.

TERIYAKI WINGS

Wonderful party or potluck food! Serves 8 as an appetizer. Serve with SWEET HOT MUSTARD, (see page 54).

1 lb. chicken wings (cut off tips and save for stock)
¼ cup soy sauce
3 Tbsp. brown sugar
½ tsp. ground ginger
2 to 3 dashes cayenne pepper
¼ cup **ORANGE VINEGAR** *or* **LEMON VINEGAR** *or* **GARLIC VINEGAR**
1 tsp. lemon juice
2 cloves garlic, peeled and mashed

Place wings in shallow pan or ziplock plastic bag. Combine all other ingredients and pour over wings. Marinate in refrigerator overnight. Drain and bake at 300 degrees for 40 minutes.

CHINESE STYLE HOT 'N SOUR SOUP

This is a delicious way to start an Oriental feast, especially when paired with grilled marinated fish fillets and cucumber salad. Makes 6 large or 8 medium-sized servings.

¼ lb. sliced lean pork steak
2 Tbsp. soy sauce
2 Tbsp. granulated sugar
1 tsp. fresh peeled minced ginger root
2 Tbsp. peanut oil
½ cup sliced fresh mushrooms
1 cup drained bamboo shoots
1 lb. drained tofu, cubed
6 cups chicken broth, fat skimmed off
¾ cup **GARLIC VINEGAR** *or* **ONION PEPPER** *or*
   GREEN ONION & PEPPERCORNS VINEGAR
½ cup soy sauce
3 Tbsp. cornstarch
salt and pepper to taste
2 eggs, beaten slightly
sliced green onion as garnish

Marinate pork in next 3 ingredients for 15 minutes. Drain well, then saute in oil over high heat in a large wok or saucepan until just cooked. Add mushrooms and shoots. Stir over heat 2 to 3 minutes then add all other ingredients except eggs and cornstarch. Combine cornstarch with a little water. Add to soup and bring to boil, stirring until thickened. Reduce to a simmer and correct seasonings with salt and pepper. Add beaten eggs slowly, stirring in well to make the "soup flowers". Serve hot in bowl, floating sliced green onions on top.

GARLIC FESTIVAL GAZPACHO WITH GARLIC VINEGAR

This chilled soup recipe was served at the Ark Garlic Festival in Nahcotta, Washington and was a hit with all the garlic-lovers on that hot June afternoon. Serves 8.

3 large tomatoes, seeded and chopped
1 green pepper, seeded and chopped
1 red (sweet) pepper, seeded and chopped
1 medium cucumber, peeled and chopped
1 cup finely chopped celery
½ cup minced green onion
2 avocados, seeded, peeled and diced
4 cups unsalted tomato juice
3 Tbsp. olive oil
5 Tbsp. **GARLIC VINEGAR**
2 cloves garlic, minced
2 tsp. salt
½ tsp. black pepper
dash cayenne pepper, if desired
sour cream, as garnish

Mix all ingredients in a large plastic or glass container. Chill overnight. Serve in large bowls or mugs: garnish with a dollop of sour cream.

OREGON BLUEBERRY CHICKEN

*This was the first recipe I developed using our **BLUEBERRY VINEGAR** and it is so exceptional that it alone is responsible for the continuing success of the business. People will mention to me months after I've served it at a demonstration how much they loved 'that chicken'. Serves 4.*

4 split-boned chicken breasts (or unboned if you prefer)
2 Tbsp. butter
¼ cup chopped onion
4 Tbsp. **BLUEBERRY VINEGAR**
¼ cup chicken stock
¼ cup sour cream
1 Tbsp. chopped tomato
fresh blueberries, if possible, for garnish

Saute chicken in butter on higher heat until golden, about 3 minutes on each side, longer if unboned. Remove chicken from pan and set aside. Reduce heat and add onion; cook until transparent, about 5 minutes. Add vinegar and raise heat until sauce is reduced to a spoonful. Whisk in stock, sour cream and tomato, simmering over lower heat for 1 minute. Return chicken to pan and simmer until well cooked, about 8 to 10 minutes. Serve at once garnished with blueberries.

Variation: OREGON BLUEBERRY CHICKEN CREPES

Serves 4 elegantly.

Prepare **OREGON BLUEBERRY CHICKEN** as directed, with these changes. Slice the uncooked chicken breasts into small slivers. Increase stock to ½ cup. Increase sour cream to ¾ cup. Increase chopped tomato to ¼ cup.

Prepare 1 dozen crepes. Divide cooked chicken evenly between crepes and roll up. Place in flat, oven-proof serving dish. Pour remaining sauce over the top and bake at 350 degrees for 20 minutes. Garnish with fresh blueberries and additional sour cream just before serving.

CHINESE CHICKEN

A regular family favorite served with brown rice and **Creamy Cucumber Salad,** *(see page* 46 *). Serves 4.*

4 chicken breasts, boned and cubed
2 Tbsp. butter
1 (20-ounce) can pineapple tidbits, drained, save juice
1/3 cup **GREEN PEPPER VINEGAR** *or* **RASPBERRY VINEGAR**
2 Tbsp. cornstarch, mixed with a little water
1/3 cup brown sugar
1 Tbsp. honey
2 Tbsp. soy sauce
1 green bell pepper
1 red bell pepper

Saute chicken in butter until browned and cooked through. Keep warm. In a pot combine saved juice, vinegar, cornstarch with water, sugar, honey and soy sauce. Cook over medium heat, stirring until thickened. Seed and slice peppers. Add pineapple, peppers and chicken to the sauce. Serve over rice.

RASPBERRY SEAFOOD SAUTE

An elegant, simple dish to show off your beautiful clear red **RASPBERRY VINEGAR.** *Serve with buttered noodles or rice. Serves 4.*

¼ cup minced onion
2 Tbsp. butter
3 Tbsp. **RASPBERRY VINEGAR**
¼ cup vegetable **or** fish stock
8 ozs. fresh tiny shrimp, cooked
8 ozs. fresh scallops
¼ cup sour cream
1 Tbsp. diced tomato
fresh raspberries, as garnish

In a large skillet or wok, saute onion in butter until transparent, about 3 to 4 minutes. Add vinegar, stock, shrimp and scallops and cook briefly, about 5 minutes, stirring often. Scallops should be opaque. Stir in sour cream over low heat; add tomato at the last minute. Serve at once. Garnish with fresh raspberries, if possible.

SPECIAL SPANISH RICE

This dish represents all the warm homey cooking you remember from childhood. This easy recipe uses vinegar to enliven the overtones of tomato. Serves 8.

2 lbs. ground beef, browned and drained
2 medium sweet onions, chopped
2 green bell peppers, seeded and chopped
1 red bell pepper, seeded and chopped
1 (28-ounce) can tomatoes
1 (8 ounce) can herbed tomato sauce
1 cup water
2 tsp. chili powder, less for a mild rice
2 tsp. salt, or to taste
1 tsp. cumin
2 tsp. Worcestershire sauce
1/3 cup **PEPPER & SPICES VINEGAR** *or* **BLACKBERRY VINEGAR** *or* **ROSEMARY VINEGAR** *or* **CHERRY VINEGAR**
1 cup uncooked brown rice

Combine all ingredients in a large oven-proof baking dish. Bake for one hour at 350 degrees.

Tip: This dish can also be frozen after cooking and reheated for 30 minutes at 350 degrees.

TENDER BEEF WITH MUSHROOMS

I like to prepare food that is easy but tastes like I spent all day in the kitchen, don't you? This recipe is a good example. Team it with fresh pasta and French bread for a dinner that is company-perfect. Serves 6.

2 lbs. cubed stew beef, trimmed of fat
2 sweet onions, sliced
2 Tbsp. brown sugar
2 cups sliced mushrooms
1 cup beef stock
½ cup **SHALLOT & GARLIC VINEGAR** *or* **THYME VINEGAR** *or* **BLUEBERRY VINEGAR**
1 cup sour cream
sliced green onions and chopped parsley, as garnish

Combine all ingredients except sour cream and garnish. Place in Dutch oven. Bake at 300 degrees for 1½ hours until beef is fork-tender. Remove from heat and stir in sour cream. Place in attractive serving dish and garnish.

EASY HAM WITH FRUIT

On a cool fall or winter evening, this recipe will fill your entire house with a marvelous aroma, drawing you into the kitchen like magic. Serve with brown rice. Makes 6 servings.

2 to 2½ lbs. boneless ham, preferably smoked
2 cups water
1 tsp. ground cloves
2 green onions, chopped
12 pitted prunes
1 carrot, scraped and sliced
1 tsp. black pepper
½ cup **RASPBERRY VINEGAR** *or* **PEACH & ANISE VINEGAR** *or* **SHALLOT VINEGAR** *or* **MANGO VINEGAR**

Put ham into Dutch oven. Mix all other ingredients in large bowl and pour over ham. Bake at 300 degrees for 2 hours.

RASPBERRY PORK CHOPS

This recipe is on the label of my OREGON RASPBERRY VINEGAR. When you taste it, you'll know why. Serves 4.

4 lean pork chops
2 Tbsp. flour, if desired
1½ Tbsp. butter
1 Tbsp. oil
6 Tbsp. **RASPBERRY VINEGAR**
¾ cup chicken broth
½ cup heavy cream

Coat chops with flour, if desired. In skillet, brown chops in butter and oil, turning once. Remove chops and add vinegar and broth to pan drippings. Stir over low heat until well combined. Return chops to pan. Simmer until cooked, about 10 minutes each side. Remove pork to a serving platter. Raise heat and boil sauce until thickened slightly, about 5 minutes. Add cream, stirring until thick. Pour over pork chops and serve at once.

Variation: For **RASPBERRY CHICKEN,** use 4 split boned chicken breasts instead of pork chops.

MARINATED PORK ROAST WITH HERBS

Easy to make, but an impressive roast to grace a special table. Serve with oven-roasted potatoes. Serves 8 generously.

2 tsp. fresh tarragon **or** 1 tsp. dried
1 Tbsp. fresh parsley **or** 1 tsp. dried
3 Tbsp. crushed dried black peppercorns, divided
½ cup **RASPBERRY VINEGAR** *or* **GREEN ONION &
   PEPPERCORNS** *or* **MIXED HERBS & SPICES
   VINEGAR**
¼ cup soy sauce
¾ cup red table wine
¼ cup water, as necessary
4 to 5 lb. pork roast (center loin cut, as lean as possible)
2 Tbsp. mustard

Combine herbs, 1 tablespoon of peppercorns, vinegar, soy sauce and wine and water in a shallow dish or a large ziplock bag. Place roast in marinade, turning well. Refrigerate for 8 hours. Turn occasionally. Drain and reserve marinade while you preheat oven to 325 degrees. Spread mustard over roast and pat on remaining peppercorns. Put in pan in the oven and pour reserved marinade around sides. Bake until meat thermometer reads 170 degrees (3 to 4 hours).

MARINATED FRESH VEGETABLES

Transform fresh vegetables with this exciting marinade.
Serves 4 to 6.

¾ cup salad oil, preferably safflower
½ cup **ANY FLAVORED VINEGAR**
2 Tbsp. lemon juice (omit if you use **LEMON VINEGAR**)
3 Tbsp. finely chopped sweet onion
1 tsp. dried tarragon
1 tsp. salt **or** salt substitute
½ Tbsp. granulated sugar, if desired (omit if using a
    SWEET FRUIT VINEGAR, like **BLACKBERRY**.)
3 to 4 cups cut-up fresh vegetables such as carrots, onion
    rings, zucchini, cherry tomatoes, pea pods, celery slices,
    diced sunchokes, broccoli, cauliflower, celery root, and
    olives.

Mix all ingredients except vegetables in a bowl using a
whisk. Pour marinade over fresh vegetables in flat shallow
container. Cover and marinate for at least 3 hours or
overnight. Drain and serve.

CARROTS SAUTEED IN BLACKBERRY VINEGAR

This simple recipe is so outstanding that I put it on the label
of my OREGON BLACKBERRY VINEGAR. You'll never
believe how sweet these carrots are! Serves 4 to 6.

4 Tbsp. butter
1 cup chopped onion
2 lbs. carrots, peeled and sliced into 'pennies'
⅓ cup **BLACKBERRY VINEGAR**
¼ cup chicken stock

Saute onion in butter, about 5 minutes, until transparent.
Add carrots, cover and cook until tender over low heat,
about 20 minutes. Add vinegar and stock. Raise heat and
stir until liquid evaporates. Serve at once.

RED APPLE CABBAGE

Hearty winter fare made to go with sliced sweet ham and mustard sauce. Serves 6.

2 tsp. salt **or** less to taste
1 cup hot chicken broth
1 Tbsp. honey
½ cup **BLUEBERRY VINEGAR** *or* **MIXED HERBS VINEGAR** *or* **SWEET BASIL VINEGAR**
3 Tbsp. butter
1 small head red cabbage, thinly sliced
1 yellow onion, thinly sliced
3 firm red apples, cored and sliced
Sour cream, as garnish

Combine salt, broth, honey, vinegar and butter in large pot. Bring to a simmer, then add cabbage, onion and apples. Stir well and simmer slowly 25 minutes. Garnish with sour cream just before serving.

GRILLED SWEET PEPPERS

This colorful but simple recipe has enough personality to stand alone as a side dish but is excellent topping sausages or hamburgers. Serves 8 as a relish.

2 red bell peppers
2 green bell peppers
2 sweet yellow peppers
2 to 3 Tbsp. olive oil
sprinkle of salt
2 to 3 Tbsp. fresh cilantro **or** basil
¼ cup **MIXED HERBS VINEGAR** *or* **RASPBERRY VINEGAR**

Seed and chop peppers into large pieces. Place in oven-proof dish. Heat oven to 425 degrees. Mix oil, salt, herb and vinegar together and pour over peppers. Place in oven for about 20 minutes. Serve hot.

CURRIED CHICKEN SALAD

In hot weather this salad is **the** *answer for a cool dinner. Team it up with a spoonful of chutney and fresh fruit for an easy but elegant meal. Serves 4.*

2 cups diced cooked chicken **or** turkey
2 cups thinly sliced celery
1 (8-ounce) can sliced water chestnuts, drained
1 (20-ounce) can pineapple tidbits, drained
1½ cups mayonnaise
2 tsp. curry powder
1 Tbsp. soy sauce
2 Tbsp. **TANGERINE VINEGAR** *or* **BLUEBERRY VINEGAR** *or* **MIXED HERBS & SPICES VINEGAR**

Combine all ingredients, stirring well. Chill for several hours to blend flavors. Serve on a bed of shredded lettuce or as a filling for pita bread.

VALERIE'S SUMMER RICE SALAD

A close friend of mine, a strict vegetarian, created this popular potluck dish. Serves 6.

3 cups cooked brown rice
¼ cup **RASPBERRY VINEGAR** *or* **OTHER VINEGAR**
    about 2 Tbsp. fresh basil **or** dill **or** tarragon*
⅓ cup chopped celery
3 green onions, chopped
½ cup sliced black olives
1 cup tiny peas, fresh **or** frozen
½ cup carrots, briefly cooked and sliced
1 cup sour cream
shredded lettuce

Combine cooled rice, vinegar and herb of choice, stirring well. Add remaining ingredients and serve chilled on a bed of lettuce.

*Note: If you have to substitute dried herbs for the fresh ones, use about 2 teaspoons.

45

CAULIFLOWER SALAD WITH SHRIMP

The use of highly colored fruit vinegar gives a nice pink tint to this salad. Serves 4 to 6.

1 head cauliflower, finely chopped
1 cup thinly sliced celery
2 Tbsp. diced onion
2 Tbsp. **RASPBERRY VINEGAR** *or* **CRANBERRY VINEGAR** *or* **BLACKBERRY VINEGAR**
½ cup mayonnaise
salt and pepper
12 ounces fresh tiny cooked shrimp
2 to 3 hard boiled eggs, as garnish

Combine all ingredients except shrimp and eggs. Chill overnight in refrigerator. Just before serving, stir in shrimp. Garnish with quartered hard-boiled eggs.

Tip: As additional garnish, if desired, mix equal quantities of mayonnaise and whipped cream. Place a dollop on top of each serving.

CREAMY CUCUMBER SALAD

This smooth, creamy dish is Scandinavian in origin. Perfect with baked fish, such as fresh Pacific Ocean salmon. Serves 4.

2 cucumbers, peeled and sliced
1 tsp. salt
1 cup sour cream
3 Tbsp. **BLACKBERRY VINEGAR** *or* **DILLED VINEGAR** *or* **PEPPER VINEGAR** *or* **ROSEMARY VINEGAR**
4 tsp. minced green onions

Sprinkle cucumbers with salt in colander and allow to drain for one hour. Rinse with clear water and drain 5 minutes. Mix sour cream, vinegar and onions in serving bowl. Add cucumber slices and refrigerate 2 to 3 hours before serving.

STEAK SALAD WITH RASPBERRY DRESSING

If you are trying to impress that special person in your life, this salad could do the trick. Add fresh french bread, unsalted butter, a good wine and forget dessert! You won't miss it. Serves 4.

½ cup oil, part olive
¼ cup **RASPBERRY VINEGAR**
¼ cup light cream **or** half-and-half (dieters: use 2% milk)
sprinkle of seasoning salt
1 egg yolk
1 tsp. mustard
1 tsp. fresh chopped tarragon **or** ¼ tsp. dried
½ head leaf lettuce, torn into bite size pieces
12 ounces thinly sliced cooked steak, medium rare
2 green onions, sliced

In top of double boiler combine oil, vinegar, cream, salt, yolk, mustard and tarragon. Whisk together over medium heat until thick. This can be done the night before as it must be cold for the salad. Keep in refrigerator. Place lettuce leaves on 4 plates, then put steak slices on top. Sprinkle with dressing and garnish with green onion.

SPINACH FETTUCINE SALAD

This makes quite a bit of salad but will keep for several days. The recipe can easily be cut in half. Serves 8 to 10.

1½ lb. fresh spinach fettucine
½ cup oil, part olive
½ cup **GARLIC VINEGAR** *or* **BASIL VINEGAR** *or*
  CHIVES & CHILI VINEGAR
2 Tbsp. chopped fresh basil
2 cloves fresh garlic, minced
½ cup chopped fresh parsley
1 (16 -ounce) can red beans, drained and rinsed
2 carrots, peeled and chopped
1 sweet onion, diced
2 hard-boiled eggs, peeled and chopped

Cook pasta as directed. Drain and rinse with cool water. Mix oil, vinegar, basil, garlic, and parsley in a bowl, stirring well. Add pasta, beans, carrots, onion and eggs and toss well. Chill several hours before serving.

ONE OF THE BEST PASTA SALADS FROM MEXICO

My parents love to get away from the Oregon rain when it is at its worst, in mid-winter, and head down to the warm climate of Mexico for a chance to see the sun. This spicy recipe came back with them. Serves 6 generously.

2 cups uncooked small pasta shells
¾ cup mayonnaise
½ cup salsa **or** taco sauce
¼ cup **GARLIC VINEGAR**
2 tsp. onion salt
1 tsp. chili powder
4 to 5 drops of Tabasco **or** red pepper sauce
2 cloves of garlic, minced
1 (16-ounce) can of kidney beans, drained
½ cup sliced black olives

Cook pasta as directed, drain and rinse. Mix mayonnaise, chili sauce, vinegar, onion salt, chili powder, hot sauce and garlic. Add pasta, beans and olives and stir well. Chill overnight or for at least 3 hours before serving.

MARINATED MUSHROOMS

For mushroom lovers this can be heaven on earth. Don't be afraid of substituting other mushroom varieties such as Chanterelles. Serves 8 as an appetizer, 4 as a side dish.

1 lb. mushrooms, cleaned and sliced ¼″ thick
1 sweet onion, thinly sliced
2 cloves garlic, minced
1 tsp. dry mustard
1 tsp. salt
1 Tbsp. granulated sugar, if desired
¼ cup water
½ cup **ONION-PEPPER VINEGAR** *or* **CHIVES & CHILI VINEGAR** *or* **GREEN ONION & PEPPERCORNS VINEGAR** *or* **RASPBERRY VINEGAR**
⅓ cup olive oil
1 Tbsp. finely chopped fresh parsley

Put sliced mushrooms into a large glass jar or bowl. Mix rest of ingredients, choosing vinegar variety for taste desired. Pour over mushrooms. Refrigerate overnight and drain before serving.

HONEY DRESSING

Such a simple name for such an extraordinarily good dressing! It adds sparkle to your fruit salads. (Remember that honey is not advisable for children under two.) Makes about 2 cups.

2/3 cup granulated sugar, optional
1 tsp. dry mustard
1 tsp. paprika
1 tsp. celery seed
1/3 cup honey, warmed to allow mixing ease
5 Tbsp. **RASPBERRY VINEGAR** *or* **CHIVE VINEGAR** *or* **PEACH VINEGAR** *or* **ONION VINEGAR**
1 tsp. grated onion
1 cup salad oil, part olive oil
½ tsp. salt
¼ tsp. pepper

In a blender combine sugar, mustard, paprika, celery seeds, honey, vinegar and onion. Add oil slowly, drop by drop while running blender at low speed. Add seasonings to taste, then chill several hours before using.

BONNE FEMME VINAIGRETTE

This basic salad dressing has many variations, depending upon your choice of vinegars. Make about 2/3 cup.

1 Tbsp. mustard, homemade **or** any Dijon type
3 Tbsp. **ANY FLAVORED VINEGAR**
½ cup salad oil, part olive, if desired

Combine mustard and vinegar in a small bowl. Add oil slowly, while whisking. You may add your favorite herbs, if desired, to enhance vinegar flavor. Adjust seasoning with salt and fresh-ground pepper.

Variation: Experiment by adding tomato juice, mayonnaise or yogurt, minced garlic or shallots, crumbled bleu cheese or sour cream to this basic recipe.

CHINESE GINGER SALAD DRESSING

Leafy lettuce topped with this piquant dressing makes a delightful introduction to an Oriental feast. Makes about 3 cups.

1 medium-sized onion, chopped into small pieces
1 medium carrot, peeled and diced
1 stalk of celery, diced
1 cup **GINGER VINEGAR** *or* **GREEN ONION VINEGAR**
1 tsp. minced fresh peeled ginger root **or** ½ tsp. ground ginger
1 cup oil (part olive if desired)
½ cup soy sauce
1 small tomato, diced
salt, pepper to taste

Place all ingredients in a blender and process on high speed until smooth. Store in refrigerator.

Tip: You may add a dash of cayenne pepper for a hotter flavor.

RASPBERRY COOLER

Oddly, this drink is not at all sour. Simply mellow and more full-bodied than regular pop. Experiment with herb vinegars for a refreshing change from iced tea. Makes 1 serving.

1 to 2 Tbsp. **RASPBERRY** *or* **OTHER VINEGAR**
ice cubes to fill tall glass
7-UP, sparkling water **or** ginger ale

Place vinegar in a tall glass, add ice cubes and fill with 7-UP, sparkling water or ginger ale. Stir and enjoy! Sugar may be added if you use sparkling water.

Tip: If using one of the herb vinegars, garnish with a fresh sprig of that herb, for example, mint leaves or parsley.

RED HOT CHILI SAUCE

When barbecuing meats and chicken, add this nippy sauce during the last 20 minutes of cooking. Makes 5 cups.

1 green bell pepper, seeded and diced
1 fresh red hot chili,* seeded and diced **or** 1 tsp. chili
    powder
2 (16-ounces) cans stewed tomatoes
1 medium onion, chopped
2 cloves garlic, minced
¼ cup olive oil
4 Tbsp. fresh chopped parsley
2 Tbsp. honey
2 Tbsp. brown sugar
2 tsp. salt
1 tsp. fresh ground pepper
¼ cup **CHIVES & CHILI   VINEGAR,** *or* **GARLIC
    VINEGAR** *or* **BLACKBERRY VINEGAR** *or* **PEPPER
    & SPICES VINEGAR**

Combine all ingredients in a large saucepan and cook over low heat for about 45 minutes, stirring frequently. Blend in food processor or blender until smooth. Store in covered jar and refrigerate.

*Variation: For those that don't like it hot, substitute a mild yellow or green pepper for the red hot pepper.

GARLIC BARBECUE SAUCE

Great over ribs or chicken! Makes about 2 cups.

6 ozs. tomato paste
1½ cups water
3 Tbsp. **GARLIC VINEGAR**
2 Tbsp. mustard
2 Tbsp. brown sugar **or** honey
1 tsp. salt
½ tsp. pepper
1 clove of garlic, minced, optional

Combine all ingredients in a small saucepan. Simmer 20 minutes, stirring often.

SWEET AND SOUR SAUCE

Pour over fried chicken wings, or deep-fried fish fillets for an Oriental treat. Serve with rice and a marinated cucumber salad. Makes about 2 cups.

2 Tbsp. cornstarch
1 (15¼ ounce) can pineapple chunks
1 green, red **or** yellow bell pepper, seeded and diced
¹/₃ cup **ORANGE VINEGAR** *or* **CHERRY VINEGAR** *or*
  GARLIC VINEGAR *or* **CHIVES & CHILI VINEGAR**
  or **CRANBERRY VINEGAR**
½ cup brown sugar
2 Tbsp. soy sauce

Mix cornstarch with a little water. Combine all ingredients in saucepan. Cook until thickened, stirring constantly, about 5 minutes over medium heat.

EASY PINK SAUCE

This recipe is so easy I'm almost embarrassed to include it. But this book wouldn't be complete without my old standby. Delicious over salads, raw or cooked vegetables, Crab or Shrimp Louis. Makes about ½ cup.

½ cup mayonnaise*
4 tsp. **RASPBERRY VINEGAR** *or* **OTHER DARK RED
  FRUIT VINEGAR, SUCH AS BLACKBERRY** *or*
  BLUEBERRY
Honey *or* sugar to sweeten, as desired

Combine all ingredients, stirring well. Refrigerate.

Variation: Substitute sour cream or yogurt for
mayonnaise.   53

SWEET HOT MUSTARD SAUCE

Team this very special mustard with a bottle of your best vinegar for a perfect gift! Makes 2²/₃ cups.

4 oz. dry mustard
1 cup **RASPBERRY VINEGAR**, *or* **HERBS & SPICES VINEGAR**, *or* **TANGERINE & CINNAMON VINEGAR**, *or* **LIME VINEGAR**
2 eggs
1 cup granulated sugar
¼ tsp. salt
1½ cups mayonnaise
1 Tbsp. grated lime peel **or** grated orange peel, optional

Mix mustard and vinegar in glass bowl and let stand, covered, overnight. Beat in eggs, sugar and salt. Cook in top of double boiler, stirring until thick. Cool, add mayonnaise, and beat well. Store in refrigerator. Use within 3 weeks.

HOMEMADE MUSTARD

A classic that makes a special gift. Makes about 2 cups.

4 oz. dry mustard (I prefer Coleman's)
2 Tbsp. sweet white wine
2 eggs, well beaten
¾ to 1 cup **RASPBERRY VINEGAR** *or* **LIME VINEGAR** *or* **DILLED GARLIC VINEGAR** *or* **APRICOT & ALLSPICE VINEGAR**
1 cup granulated sugar

Combine all ingredients stirring well. Store in refrigerator.

LIME MARINADE

Marinate firm white fish fillets before grilling over hot coals. Also delicious with fresh vegetables. Makes about 1½ cups.

¹/₃ cup **LIME VINEGAR**
1 tsp. salt
½ cup salad oil, part olive
1 small lime, thinly sliced
½ cup white wine
2 Tbsp. fresh parsley, chopped

Combine all ingredients in small deep bowl, beating until well blended. Marinate fish or vegetables in refrigerator for several hours before grilling.

SHALLOT MARINADE

Create exciting, yet easy vegetable salads with SHALLOT MARINADE. Tenderize less expensive cuts of meat, such as round steak by marinating 3 to 4 hours in refrigerator; then broil or barbecue. Makes about 1¾ cups.

¾ cup salad oil, part olive
¾ cup **SHALLOT VINEGAR** *or* **OTHER VINEGAR OF CHOICE**
3 Tbsp. shallots, finely chopped
1 Tbsp. fresh parsley **or** basil, finely chopped
1 tsp. salt
½ tsp. ground black pepper

Mix all ingredients in small deep bowl, beating until well blended.

OREGON CRANBERRY CHUTNEY

This recipe is featured on my bottles of OREGON CRANBERRY VINEGAR. I can't recall the number of times someone has asked me at a demonstration where they could buy this wonderful chutney! You can make it yourself very easily, using any variety of vinegar you prefer.

1 cup **CRANBERRY VINEGAR** or substitute
2 cups sugar
2 tsp. ground ginger
1 tsp. ground cloves
¼ tsp. chili powder
5-6 drops hot pepper sauce
1 tsp. salt
2 garlic cloves, minced
2 cups whole cranberries, ground in blender with part of
    vinegar for liquid
3-4 medium tart apples, peeled, cored and diced
1 cup chopped nuts (almonds, pecans, **or** walnuts)

Mix first nine ingredients in large stainless steel pot with lid. Heat to boiling, stirring constantly, then add apples. Simmer 30 minutes or until thick, stirring occasionally. Add nuts and cool. Store in refrigerator for up to 4 weeks or freeze up to six months. A beautiful red spicy chutney, perfect with roast meats, cream cheese or crackers.

PAPAYA CHUTNEY

Delicious and exotic with roasted meats or fried rice dishes. Also good on sandwiches and hamburgers. Mix with cream cheese for an exceptional spread on nut breads or crackers. Makes about 6 cups.

1 cup **MINT & CLOVES VINEGAR,** *or* **PEPPER & SPICES VINEGAR** *or* **APRICOT AND ALLSPICE VINEGAR**
1½ cups granulated sugar
1 tsp. ground allspice
1 tsp. ground cloves
1 tsp. salt
7 to 8 cups cubed peeled papaya
1 hot green chili pepper, seeded and chopped
1 clove garlic, minced
1½ Tbsp. peeled ginger root, finely chopped
1 cup seedless raisins
¼ cup chopped toasted almonds, optional

Boil vinegar and sugar together in stainless steel or enamel pot. Add spices and cook 5 minutes. Add papaya, pepper, garlic, ginger, raisins and almonds. Simmer until thick, about 20 minutes, stirring frequently to prevent scorching. Pour into hot clean jars and seal. Process for 10 minutes in a hot water bath.

PETER'S PICKLED PEPPERS

Here is a gourmet gift that's guaranteed to please; beautiful jars of red, green, and yellow peppers. Makes 1 quart.

4 green bell peppers
4 red bell peppers
4 yellow sweet peppers
1 cup small onions, peeled
3 cups **CHILI PEPPER VINEGAR, PEPPER VINEGAR** *or* **LEMON VINEGAR**
1 cup salad oil, preferably part olive oil
1 Tbsp. salt **or** salt substitute

Wash and seed peppers. Chop peppers and onions into large pieces. Put vinegar, oil and salt into an enamel or stainless steel pot. Bring to a boil; then add peppers and onions. Cook 6 to 7 minutes. Remove from heat; cool. Store in jars in refrigerator a week before eating. Keeps 1 month, refrigerated.

SPECIAL BREAD AND BUTTER PICKLES

Select your favorite vinegar to make these all-purpose pickles. Makes about 6 quarts.

6 qt. sliced medium cucumbers
6 medium sweet onions, sliced
1 cup salt
1½ qts. **CHIVES & CHILI VINEGAR,** *or* **SHALLOT & GARLIC VINEGAR,** *or* **DILLED ONION VINEGAR** *or* **MIXED HERBS & SPICES VINEGAR**
6 cups granulated sugar
½ cup mustard seed
2 Tbsp. celery seed
1 Tbsp. whole green peppercorns
6 drops Tabasco sauce

Put sliced cucumbers and onions into large crock with salt. Let stand 3 hours. Place in colander. Drain liquid and rinse away extra salt with cold water. Combine all other ingredients and boil in large stainless steel or enamel pot, adding cucumbers and onions a few at a time. Simmer 4 to 5 minutes, stirring gently, then pack into clean jars and seal. Process in hot water bath 15 minutes.

PEPPER-FLAVORED PICCALILLI

If you ever have a summer like we do here in Oregon where tomatoes stay green until the snow falls, try this recipe to use them up. Save a few jars, if you can, for Christmas presents. Makes about 8 quarts.

25 to 30 lbs. green tomatoes, diced
1 dozen large sweet onions, peeled and chopped
1 cup salt
2 qts. **PLAIN VINEGAR**
2 qts. water, divided
2½ qts. **GREEN PEPPER VINEGAR** *or* **CHIVES & CHILI VINEGAR**
6 lbs. granulated sugar
4 to 6 Tbsp. whole pickling spices

Place tomatoes and onions in large bowl, sprinkle with salt and let stand overnight. Next morning, strain tomatoes and onions in colander. Place in large stainless steel or enamel pot, then add the 2 quarts plain white vinegar and 1 quart of the water. Boil slowly for 45 minutes. Strain again and return to kettle, adding the flavored vinegar, 1 quart water, sugar and spices. Bring to a boil, reduce heat and simmer slowly for 1½ hours, stirring frequently. Pour into clean jars, seal and process in hot water bath 15 minutes.

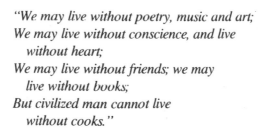

"We may live without poetry, music and art;
We may live without conscience, and live
without heart;
We may live without friends; we may
live without books;
But civilized man cannot live
without cooks."

Owen Meredith

INDEX

Sauces

Soups

Vegetables

Vinegars

MAIL-ORDER RESOURCE

Quality white and red wine vinegars that are excellent for making the gourmet vinegars in this book, as well as mustard making items, may be ordered by mail from the following source. Request a price list from:

Gazzelle's Fine Foods
P.O. Box 980
Canby, OR 97013-0980
(503) 266-4140